Grades 4-5

SCHOLASTIC

Instant Grammar Practice Kids Will Love!

Linda Ward Beech

New York • Toronto • London • Auckland • Sydney
Mexico City • New Delhi • Hong Kong • Buenos Aires

Teaching *Resources*

Previously published as *Ready-to-Go Reproducibles: Great Grammar Skill Builders: Grades 4–5*

Cover design by Maria Lilja
Interior design by Solutions by Design, Inc.
Cover and interior illustrations by Mike Moran

ISBN-13: 978-0-545-23970-7
ISBN-10: 0-545-23970-2

To the Teacher

Many students have difficulty with grammar in both oral and written language, but because grammar is a basic tool of communication, it is essential that they master these concepts. The pages in this book offer students practice and reinforcement. More important, these pages provide opportunities to use grammar concepts in appealing writing assignments. You can use these reproducibles to:

* supplement your language-arts curriculum.

* expand your writing program.

* create instant homework sheets.

* teach, reteach, or review essential skills.

* provide practice needed for mastery.

Using This Book

* Look over the table of contents to determine which pages meet the needs of your students.

* Read aloud the instructions and answer students' inquiries.

* If necessary, model the activity. In some cases, you may want to do the first item with the class.

* Use the Student Assessment Chart on page 5 to record student progress.

Page by Page

Here are some suggestions for supporting learning.

Page 6 Point out that the main verb always appears in the predicate of a sentence.

Page 7 Have students explain why the sentences in item 2 are incomplete.

Page 9 Caution students not to overuse exclamation points in writing. Tell them that the punctuation for these sentences will depend on their interpretation of the sentences.

Page 10 Be sure students use the lowercase for the first word after the comma.

Page 11 Discuss the rules that students write.

Page 12 Review the kinds of sentences used in the riddles.

Page 13 Have students identify the subjects of their sentences.

Page 14 Encourage students to be imaginative in the nouns they use.

Page 15 Ask students to explain why they capitalized each proper noun.

Page 16 Let students tell how they determined which words are not nouns.

Page 20 Have students use each verb in a sentence.

Page 21 Remind students to "test" each word both as a noun and a verb before proceeding.

Page 22 Point out that the verbs with –*ing* endings are used with helping verbs (in this case a form of *be*).

Page 23 Have students underline the verb in each predicate twice.

Page 24 If students use the past tense, help them reword their sentences in the present tense.

Pages 25–26 Ask students to identify which of the verbs have irregular past-tense forms.

Page 27 Have students write the present and past tense of each verb they use.

Page 28 Tell students to circle the words that each verb links.

Page 30 Encourage students to use adjectives in imaginative ways.

Page 31 Have students identify the adjectives that follow linking verbs.

Page 33 Point out that writers also use verbs and other parts of speech in descriptions.

Page 34 Explain that *good*, *better*, and *best* are irregular adjective forms.

Page 36 Talk about adverbs that end in –*ly*.

Page 37 Have students identify the verbs and adverbs they use.

Page 38 Discuss subject and object pronouns.

Page 41 Have students identify the prepositions.

Page 43 Tell students to write the abbreviations for all the months.

Page 47 Ask students to identify the singular and plural possessives they write.

Student's Name _____ 5

	Worksheet Results	Comments
Sentences		
Statements/Questions		
Exclamations/ Commands		
Subjects/ Predicates		
Capital Letters/ End Punctuation		
Sentence Writing Skills		
Parts of Speech		
Nouns		
Verbs		
Adjectives		
Adverbs		
Pronouns		
Mechanics		
Capital Letters		
Commas		
Quotation Marks		
Apostrophes		

Name_____ Date _____

Parts of a Sentence

Add three subjects and three predicates to the table below. Then use the subjects and predicates to write eight sentences. Write four that make sense and four that seem silly.

A sentence is a group of words that expresses a complete thought. The subject tells who or what did something. The predicate tells what happened.

SUBJECTS	PREDICATES
The exhausted athletes	responded to the cheers of the crowd.

1. _____

2. _____

3. _____

4. _____

5. _____

6. _____

7. _____

8. _____

➤ *Underline each subject in red and each predicate in blue.*

Instant Grammar Practice Kids Will Love! Grades 4–5 Copyright © 2000, 2010 by Linda Ward Beech, Scholastic Teaching Resources

Name_____ Date_____

Sentence or Not?

Read what each character is saying. Put a star (*) next to each incomplete sentence. Then write complete sentences for the characters who are not saying anything.

A complete sentence has a subject and a predicate and makes sense.

1. This armor is heavy.

2. Not a nice knight.   Roared at me.

3.

4. That dragon has hot breath.

➤ *Add the missing part to each incomplete sentence above.*

Name_____ Date_____

Questions and Answers

Find the statement that answers each question. Then rewrite each sentence in the table, using the correct punctuation and capitalization.

A statement tells something. It begins with a capital letter and ends with a period.

A question asks something. It begins with a capital letter and ends with a question mark.

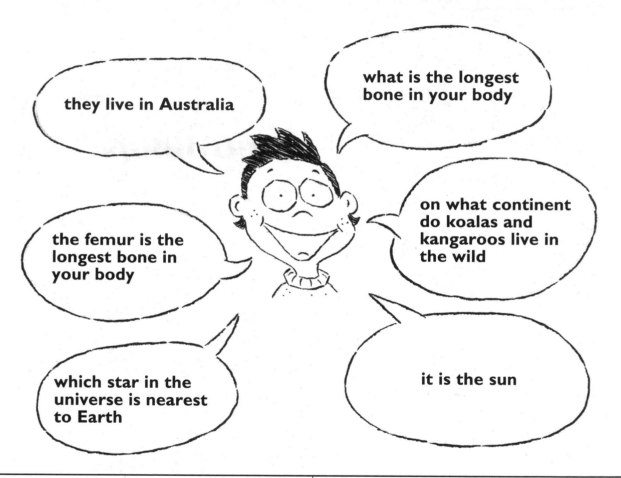

QUESTIONS	ANSWERS
1.	
2.	
3.	

➤ *Proofread your sentences to make sure you have capitalized and punctuated them correctly.*

8

Name _____ Date _____

Exclamations and Commands

Rewrite each sentence using correct capitalization and the punctuation you think is best to show an exclamation or a command.

An exclamation shows strong feeling. It begins with a capital letter and ends with an exclamation point.

A command tells someone to do something. A command begins with a capital letter and ends with a period or an exclamation point. (The subject in a command is usually left out.)

1. there's an elephant in our yard

_____

2. you're kidding

_____

3. call the fire department

_____

4. get my camera

_____

5. keep the dog inside

_____

6. hand me those binoculars

_____

7. that's quite a surprise

_____

8. he's sitting on my flowers

_____

➤ *Read aloud your sentences to a partner. Can she or he tell by your voice whether or not the sentence ends with an exclamation point?*

Name_____ Date _____

Two-in-One Sentences

Combine each pair of sentences to form a compound sentence. Add a comma before the words *and*, *but*, and *or*.

> A compound sentence is formed by connecting two simple sentences with a comma and the word *and*, *but*, or *or*.

TWO SENTENCES

ONE SENTENCE

The harp seal pup has white fur. Adult seals have gray and brown fur.

1. _____

_____

Elephant seals weigh up to 8,000 pounds. They can be as long as 23 feet.

2. _____

_____

Hippos are land animals. They live in the water most of the day.

3. _____

_____

The killer whale may feed on smaller sea mammals. It may eat other whales.

4. _____

_____

African elephants make rumbling noises to communicate. They remain silent to warn of danger.

5. _____

_____

Female lions do the family hunting. The males defend the group's territory.

6. _____

_____

➤ *Write three compound sentences of your own.*

Name_____ Date _____

Rules for Writing

Use what you know about grammar to describe the rule that tells what kind of sentence it is. Then explain the punctuation rule being used.

1. Some people combine relaxing and learning on vacations.

   Sentence rule: _____

   Punctuation rule: _____

2. That's such a great idea!

   Sentence rule: _____

   Punctuation rule: _____

3. Hawaii is a beautiful vacation spot, and you can learn about dolphins there.

   Sentence rule: _____

   Punctuation rule: _____

4. Read this brochure.

   Sentence rule: _____

   Punctuation rule: _____

5. Where would you like to spend a vacation?

   Sentence rule: _____

   Punctuation rule: _____

➤ *Write a rule about how sentences begin.*

Instant Grammar Practice Kids Will Love! Grades 4–5 Copyright © 2000, 2010 by Linda Ward Beech, Scholastic Teaching Resources

Name_____ Date _____

Sentences in Riddles

You can use different kinds of sentences in riddles. Identify each kind of sentence in the riddles below. Then write a complete sentence to answer the riddles.

1. I come in a square package, but I am round.   _____

I contain lots of information for your computer.   _____

Handle me carefully.   _____

What am I?   _____

Answer: _____

2. I have legs and arms.   _____

I have a back, too.   _____

I am not alive.   _____

What am I?   _____

Answer: _____

3. Now write your own riddle. Describe something without naming it. How many different kinds of sentences can you use?

_____

_____

_____

_____

➤ *Have a friend solve your riddle. Ask him or her to identify the different kinds of sentences you used.*

Name_____ Date _____

Knowing Nouns

A. The students in Ms. Frank's class are dressed as nouns. Can you identify them?

> A noun is a word that names a person, place, thing, or animal.

1.

_____

2.

_____

3.

_____

4.

_____

5.

_____

6.

_____

B. Use each of the nouns you identified in a sentence.

7. _____

8. _____

9. _____

10. _____

11. _____

12. _____

➤ *Fold a piece of paper in fourths. Draw a picture to illustrate each of these nouns:* sandwich, radio, earring, backpack.

Name_____ Date_____

What Nouns Name

Read the story below. Supply nouns for each
symbol in the story. Then write an ending.

> Nouns name people, places,
> things, or animals.

Key: ☆ = person   ⑥ = place
🌀 = thing   💥 = animal

Once there lived a wise 💥 _____ in a lovely, green ⑥ _____ .

All around there were tall 🌀 _____s and sparkling 🌀 _____s.

When a strange ☆ _____ came by on a 💥 _____ , the wise 💥 _____

bowed and said, "Welcome. Where are you from, and how may I help you?"

Politely came the answer: "I come from ⑥ _____ , far over the

⑥ _____ . I am here to find a rare 🌀 _____ to bring to my ☆ _____ ."

"You must go to ⑥ _____ then. Seek the ☆ _____ there.

Be sure to offer a fine 🌀 _____ in return. And beware of the other

☆ _____ and their 💥 _____s."

_____

_____

_____

_____

_____

➤ *Read aloud your story to the class. How many nouns can your classmates identify?*

Instant Grammar Practice Kids Will Love! Grades 4–5 Copyright © 2000, 2010 by Linda Ward Beech, Scholastic Teaching Resources

Name_____ Date _____

Happy Birthday Nouns

Use the information on the calendar to complete the sentences below. Use capital letters for proper nouns correctly.

Proper nouns are the special names for people, places, animals, or things. Begin a proper noun with a capital letter. (The nouns for days, months, and holidays are proper nouns.)

february

sunday	monday	tuesday	wednesday	thursday	friday	saturday
	1 jerry spinelli	2	3	4	5	6 babe ruth
7 laura ingalls wilder	8	9	10 e.l. konigsburg	11	12 judy blume	13
14 valentine's day	15	16	17	18	19	20
21	22 george washington	23	24	25 cynthia voigt	26	27
28						

1. _____ is a big month for birthdays and other celebrations.

2. The following authors have birthdays in this month: _____

_____ .

3. The famous baseball player, _____ , was born on the 6th.

4. Our nation's first president _____ was born in _____ , too.

5. The holiday _____ falls on a _____ .

6. The first day of the month is a _____ .

➤ *Underline each letter on the calendar that should be capitalized in red.*

Name_____ Date _____

Noun Treasure Hunt

Start at the arrow. Draw a line to connect the
words that are nouns. You can go across or down.
Then use the nouns to complete the sentences.

> The subject of a sentence
> is usually a noun.

→ ship	clouds	what	her	loudly
it	pirates	map	captain	rats
through	for	slow	and	birds
men	island	coast	outlaws	days
treasure	shy	cool	across	floated

1. A rundown _____ set sail one night.

2. Dark _____ concealed its departure.

3. _____ were aboard!

4. An old _____ guided their voyage.

5. The _____ roared orders.

6. Below deck, the _____ ran for cover.

7. Large _____ circled overhead.

8. _____ passed.

9. The _____ grew cranky.

10. Then a _____ appeared.

11. An _____ came into view.

12. The greedy _____ went ashore.

13. _____ was on their minds.

➤ *Write an ending to the story. Share it with the class.*

Instant Grammar Practice Kids Will Love! Grades 4–5 Copyright © 2000, 2010 by Linda Ward Beech, Scholastic Teaching Resources

Name_____ Date _____

Nouns With Endings

Complete the menu for the class party. Write the correct plural for each word in parentheses.

A plural noun names more than one person, place, thing, or animal. To form the plural, add -s to the end of most nouns. If a noun ends in *sh, ch, x, s,* or *ss,* add -*es*. In nouns that end in a consonant and *y*, change the *y* to *i*, then add -*es*.

Party Menu

Four kinds of (sandwich) _____

Salad with (cucumber) _____
and (radish) _____

Three kinds of (cheese) _____

(Bunch) _____ of grapes

Nut (mix) _____

Three hot (dish) _____

Fruit salad with (peach) _____,
(berry) _____, and (apple) _____

Assorted (cookie) _____ and
(candy) _____

Two (punch) _____

➤ *Write a review of the menu. Use plural nouns.*

Name_____ Date _____

Puzzling Plurals

Complete the puzzle. Write the plural form of each noun clue.

Some nouns have irregular plural forms. For most nouns ending in *f* or *fe*, change the *f* or *fe* to *v* and add *-es* to form the plural.

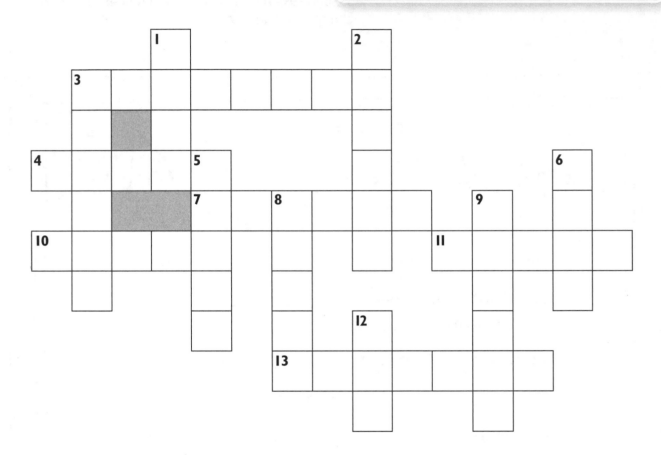

ACROSS
3. child
4. elf
7. half
10. goose
11. woman
13. shelf

DOWN
1. mouse
2. knife
3. calf
5. sheep
6. ox
7. life
9. loaf
12. man

 Write two sentences using irregular plural nouns.

Name_____ Date _____

Nouns in a Story

Look at each group of nouns. What topic do the nouns describe? Write the topic in the table. Then choose one topic and write a story about it. Use the nouns in your story.

NOUNS	TOPIC
1. grape, plum, amethyst, eggplant	
2. cradle, bunk, hammock, crib	
3. ribbon, curler, barrette, headband	
4. towel, basket, umbrella, lotion	
5. clogs, moccasins, slippers, sandals	

_____

_____

_____

_____

_____

_____

_____

_____

➤ *Reread your story. Underline all the common nouns. Circle all the proper nouns.*

Name_____ Date _____

Verbs in Action

Help these verbs spring into action!
Read each sentence. Then draw a picture
to show the action of the underlined verb.

A verb is a word that shows what someone or something does. Most verbs show action.

fall

look

1. The students <u>wiggle</u> in their seats.

4. Someone <u>drops</u> a pencil.

2. Some boys <u>tilt</u> their chairs backward.

5. A girl <u>points</u> to the clock.

3. Two kids <u>doze</u> in the back row.

6. The students <u>dash</u> to lunch.

➤ *Show your pictures to a friend. Have her or him guess and write the verbs.*

Name_____ Date _____

What's the Use?

Find three words across, down, or diagonally that you can use as either a noun or a verb. Draw a line through the words. Then use each of the words as a verb in a sentence.

> The meaning of a word often depends on how it is used. Some words can be used as both verbs and nouns.

love	went	like
cat	wave	girl
boy	seem	stare

1. _____

2. _____

3. _____

help	glass	over
follow	eraser	sidewalk
smile	spot	guess

4. _____

5. _____

6. _____

➤ *Write a sentence using each of the six words as a noun.*

Name_____ Date_____

Right Now

Use a present-tense verb to complete each sentence.

Present-tense verbs tell about action taking place now.

I am singing.

That bird sings.

1.
We are _____.

2.
I _____ after school.

3.

I _____ carefully.

4.
That cat _____.

5.
You are _____ in my ear.

6.
It is _____.

➤ Write two sentences using verbs in the present tense.

Name_____ Date _____

Agreeable Verbs

Find a match for each puzzle piece.
Then write the complete sentence.

The subject and verb in a sentence must agree.

Example:
Nina celebrates many holidays.
(A singular subject takes a singular verb.)
The neighbors celebrate many holidays.
(A plural subject takes a plural verb.)

Subject

Election Day

Every Thanksgiving, my grandma

On New Year's, Nick

Every fall, students

On the Fourth of July, I

Predicate

return to school.

comes in November.

march in a parade.

wears a silly hat.

roasts a turkey.

1. _____
2. _____
3. _____
4. _____
5. _____

➤ *Underline the singular subjects.*

Name_____ Date_____

Pairs in the Present

Look at the picture pairs. Describe what the pairs have in common. Then tell how to use each pair. Use the present tense.

1.

_____

_____

_____

_____

_____

3.

_____

_____

_____

_____

_____

2.

_____

_____

_____

_____

4.

_____

_____

_____

_____

➤ *Underline each present-tense verb you used.*

Name_____ Date _____

Puzzle in the Past

Write the past tense of each verb to complete the puzzle.

> Past-tense verbs show action that happened in the past. Add -d or -ed to form the past tense of most verbs. Some verbs have irregular past-tense forms.

ACROSS
- **3.** find
- **5.** become
- **6.** win
- **7.** cut
- **8.** utter
- **12.** dig
- **13.** dress
- **14.** date

DOWN
- **1.** go
- **2.** give
- **4.** dot
- **5.** buy
- **7.** choose
- **9.** tell
- **10.** ride
- **11.** draw
- **12.** do

➤ Write three sentences using three of the past-tense verbs from the puzzle.

Name_____ Date _____

Yesterday's News

The story below is written in the present tense, but the events it describes happened yesterday. Circle all the verbs. Then rewrite the story using the past tense.

MOOSE IN TOWN

A large moose visits Clearview this week according to Judy Cross. Ms. Cross sees the moose from her kitchen window. She calls the ranger headquarters at the state park and gives a description of the animal and tells her address.

Meanwhile the moose pushes open her garden gate and tramples over the vegetables. The tomatoes fall down, and some corn stalks break.

When the rangers come, the noise of their truck scares the moose. It runs away and disappears into the woods.

_____

_____

_____

_____

_____

_____

_____

_____

_____

➤ *Write a few sentences telling what the moose did when it reached the woods.*

Name_____ Date_____

Plans for a Play

Complete this school fair poster. Add verbs in the future tense to show what everyone will do. Use a different verb for each performer.

Future-tense verbs tell about action that will happen in the future. Use the word *will* with a verb to show the future tense.

Come to Our School Fair!

Buster _____ a bone on his nose.

Jack _____ his unicycle.   Lily _____ magic tricks.

Marcus _____ prizes.   Heather _____ popcorn and drinks.

➤ *Think of two or more things to add to the poster.*

Name_____ Date _____

The Linking Game

Play the linking game. Which subjects, linking verbs, and predicate nouns and adjectives go together? Build sentences by joining the subjects below to linking verbs and predicate nouns and adjectives.

Some verbs do not show action. Instead, they link, or join, the subject of a sentence to an adjective or noun in the predicate.

The verb *to be* is a linking verb. Forms of *to be* include *am, is, are, was,* and *were.*

Subjects	Linking Verbs	Predicate Nouns and Adjectives
This actor	am	talented.
His roles	is	demanding.
That play	are	a bit hit.
Those movies	was	the critic's favorite.
Many fans	were	teenagers.
One award		really special.
A few fans		disappointed.
Acting		a real challenge.

I am an actor. My fans are terrific.

1._____

2._____

3._____

4._____

5._____

6._____

7._____

8._____

➤ *Reread your sentences. Check to see if you linked the subjects with adjectives or nouns in the predicate.*

Name_____ Date _____

Verbs in Verse

Read the verses below. Replace the underlined words with more interesting verbs.

A hippo by the name of Old Gert

<u>Moved</u> around quite a bit in the dirt.   1. _____

She <u>went</u> this way and that way   2. _____

On every single day

And <u>said</u>, "It's fun, and it does not hurt."   3. _____

A lion by the name of Lee

<u>Sat</u> comfortably in a tree.   4. _____

He <u>made noise</u> by the hour   5. _____

From his leafy green tower

Then <u>left</u> when the coast was free.   6. _____

Write your own verse. Underline the verbs you use.

_____

_____

_____

_____

_____

_____

➤ *Read your verse to a friend. Have him or her identify the verbs you used.*

Name_____ Date _____

Adding Adjectives

Complete the triangles by adding an adjective to each line to describe the noun. Use the example below as a guide.

An adjective is a word that describes a noun. An adjective often tells what kind or how many.

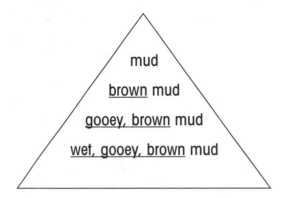

1.
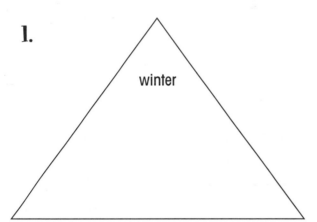

2.
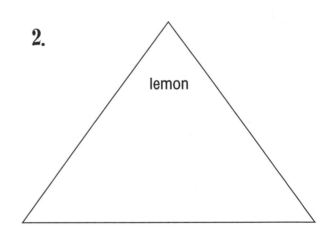

3.
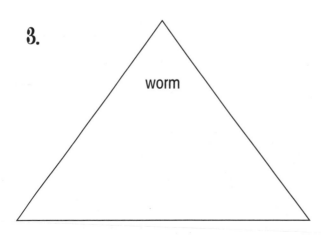

4.
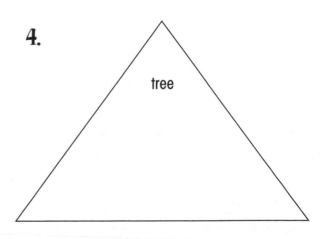

➤ *Write a sentence using the noun and all the adjectives from one of the triangles you completed.*

Name_____ Date _____

Adjectives at Work

Which noun or pronoun does each underlined
adjective describe? Write it below.

> An adjective is a word that
> describes a noun or pronoun.

The pale moon shed a shimmering light over the vast field. The plowed
earth looked forlorn in the wavering glow. An autumnal wind rustled
the leftover cornstalks. Along the field's edge, barren trees created stark
silhouettes against the mottled sky. An owl's distinctive cry filled the night. My
senses were alert; I was ready for drama. Suddenly, from across the field I saw
dark figures gliding swiftly into the forest. Behind them rang the eerie call of
coyotes, hungry enemies to the deer. What tense drama took place there in
the woods, I didn't know. Chilly, I headed for home, where a blazing fire and a
good friend awaited.

1. pale _____

2. shimmering _____

3. vast _____

4. plowed _____

5. forlorn _____

6. wavering _____

7. autumnal _____

8. leftover _____

9. barren _____

10. stark _____

11. mottled _____

12. distinctive _____

13. alert _____

14. ready _____

15. dark _____

16. eerie _____

17. hungry _____

18. tense _____

19. chilly _____

20. blazing _____

➤ *Write three adjectives to describe the mood of the paragraph above.*

Name_____ Date _____

Adjective Clues

Mr. Loosit is always misplacing things. The pictures show some of the things he is missing. Help Mr. Loosit make a list for the Lost and Found bulletin board. Add two adjectives to describe each thing.

1. _____ **mug**

2. _____ **tie**

3. _____ **shirt**

4. _____ **sock**

5. _____ **sunglasses**

6. _____ **clock**

Write a story about some of the other things Mr. Loosit has lost. Describe each thing.

_____

_____

_____

_____

_____

_____

➤ *Ask a friend to draw a picture of the things Mr. Loosit has lost, based upon the descriptions in your story.*

Instant Grammar Practice Kids Will Love! Grades 4–5 Copyright © 2000, 2010 by Linda Ward Beech, Scholastic Teaching Resources

Name_____ Date _____

Imaginative Adjective Fun

Write a complete sentence to describe each of the following things *without* using the adjectives in parentheses.

Good writers vary the adjectives they use. They also use adjectives in different and unexpected ways to paint vivid pictures with words.

1. sun (yellow, hot) _____

_____

2. pillow (soft, fluffy) _____

_____

3. puppy (small, clumsy) _____

_____

4. ice cream (smooth, delicious) _____

_____

5. ocean (wet, deep) _____

_____

6. candle (dripping, glowing) _____

_____

➤ *Underline all the adjectives you used.*

Name_____ Date _____

Good Judgment

Which cake will win the contest?
Help the judges complete their report.

> To compare two things, you usually add -*er* to an adjective. To compare three or more things, you usually add -*est* to an adjective. With long adjectives, you often use the word *more* to compare two things and the word *most* to compare three or more things.

CAKE 1   CAKE 2   CAKE 3

JUDGES' REPORT

Cake 1 is high, but Cake 2 is _____ , and Cake 3 is the

_____ of all. Cake 2 is delicious and Cake 1 is even _____ ,

but Cake 3 is the _____ . The decorations on Cake 1 are elaborate,

but there are _____ decorations on Cake 3. Even so, Cake 2 has

the _____ decorations of them all. The icing on Cake 1 is

_____ . However, the icing on Cake 3 is even _____ ,

and the icing on Cake 2 is the _____ of all the cakes.

► *Describe which cake should win the contest. Use the adjectives* good, better, *and* best *to compare the cakes.*

Adjective Poem

You can use adjectives to write a poem like the one shown below. Choose a noun with at least six letters. Write the word vertically so that each letter starts a new line. Use the letters to begin each line of the poem.

Dainty and daring

Awesome entertainer

Natural grace

Captivating

Electric

Rhythm

_____

_____

_____

_____

_____

_____

_____

➤ *Read aloud your poem to a friend. Have him or her identify the adjectives you used.*

Name_____ Date _____

Describing Verbs

Choose a verb and an adverb from the bush to
complete each sentence. Use the key to help you.
Be sure that each sentence makes sense.

An adverb is a word that describes a
verb by telling where, when, or how
an action happens.

Key: = verb   = adverb

1. Everyone _____ _____ at the family picnic.

2. Dad _____ _____ .

3. Amy _____ the juice _____ .

4. Grandpa _____ _____ with his camera.

5. The baby _____ _____ .

6. The dog _____ _____ at a squirrel.

7. Uncle Fred _____ for a walk _____ .

8. Mom _____ the cake _____ .

➤ *Circle all the adverbs that tell* how.

Name_____ Date _____

Sentence Steps

Complete each sentence step. First add a verb to the subject. Then add an adverb to build each sentence. Look at the example at the right.

Example:

| Swans |
| Swans glide. |
| Swans glide gracefully. |

1.

| Turkeys |
| |
| |

2.

| Penguins |
| |
| |

3.

| Robins |
| |
| |

4.

| Ducks |
| |
| |

5.

| Geese |
| |
| |

6.

| Hens |
| |
| |

7.

| Parrots |
| |
| |

8.

| Vultures |
| |
| |

➤ *Think of an adjective to describe each of the subjects in your completed sentences.*

Instant Grammar Practice Kids Will Love! Grades 4–5 Copyright © 2000, 2010 by Linda Ward Beech, Scholastic Teaching Resources

Name_____ Date _____

Pronoun Riddle

Choose the correct pronoun to complete each sentence. Then use the circled letters to solve the following riddle:

> A pronoun is a word that can take the place of a noun.

If it takes 3 minutes to boil 1 egg, how many minutes does it take to boil 3 eggs?

(they, them) 1. ◯ __ __ __ gave Terry a book about the Internet.

(he, him) 2. Yesterday ◯ __ sent an e-mail.

(she, her) 3. Bart told __ __ ◯ about a special offer.

(me, I) 4. Marta asked __ ◯ for Sue's address.

(she, her) 5. __ __ ◯ is designing a Web page.

(he, him) 6. The search gave __ __ ◯ a good Web site.

(me, I) 7. Bart and ◯ will look for information.

(we, us) 8. The computer helps ◯ __ in many ways.

(it, I) 9. __ ◯ is a very useful tool.

(they, them) 10. Terry and Marta use __ __ ◯ __ for work and fun.

(we, us) 11. Computers can connect __ ◯ to other people.

Answer: __ __ __ __ __   __ __ n __ __ __ __
         1 2 3 4 5   6 7   8 9 10 11

➤ *Write three sentences of your own using a different pronoun in each sentence.*

Name_____ Date _____

Great Substitutes

Read the story below. Then rewrite it using a pronoun for each underlined noun or nouns.

My family and the Riley family went on a camping trip. <u>My family and the Riley family</u> spent three nights in Green Tree Park. <u>Green Tree Park</u> is a beautiful place.

Dad was in charge of the meals. <u>Dad</u> loves to cook outdoors. As a result, <u>my family and the Riley family</u> ate very well. The meals were a treat. The group looked forward to <u>the meals</u> every day.

Mrs. Riley led the group on long hikes. <u>Mrs. Riley</u> took <u>the hikers</u> to a different place each day.

Seth told stories around the campfire at night. <u>Seth</u> told <u>the stories</u> in a scary voice. The small children were afraid to sit near <u>Seth</u>!

_____

_____

_____

_____

_____

_____

_____

_____

_____

► *Reread the story. Make sure the pronouns you used make sense.*

Name_____ Date _____

Words of Where

How many stars can you find? They are hidden
around the park. Add a preposition from the box
to each clue to tell where the stars are.

> A preposition often helps tell
> where something is.

between	on	under	against
behind	in	over	around

Clues:

1. _____ a bench

2. _____ a sand pail

3. _____ the baby's stroller

4. _____ two litter baskets

5. _____ the corner

6. _____ the fence

7. _____ Keith's foot

8. _____ the tree

➤ *The clues are prepositional phrases. Use each prepositional phrase in a sentence.*

Instant Grammar Practice Kids Will Love! Grades 4–5 Copyright © 2000, 2010 by Linda Ward Beech, Scholastic Teaching Resources

Name_____ Date _____

Building Better Sentences

Add two prepositional phrases to each sentence to tell *where* and *when*.

A preposition can tell where something is or when something happens.

Example:

| We visited Niagara Falls. |
| We visited Niagara Falls on our trip. |
| We visited Niagara Falls on our trip to Canada. |

on time	from the station	in Honolulu
at six	before noon	between here and there
by the park	on the hour	within seconds

1. The train left.

2. Our plane arrived.

3. Most ferries cross the river.

4. The bus stops.

➤ *Underline the prepositional phrases that tell* when, *and circle the prepositional phrases that tell* where.

Name_____ Date _____

Long Lists

The Long family is getting ready for a party. There's a lot to do! Write a list for each person. Use complete sentences.

A comma is a punctuation mark that shows a reader where to pause. It helps separate words and ideas. When writing a list of three or more items, use a comma between each item and before the word *and*.

1.

supermarket
bakery
fruit stand
party store

I must stop at the _____

2.

string the lights
buy extra ice
set up tables

I need to _____

3.

hairdresser
shoemaker
cleaners

I'll go to the _____

4.

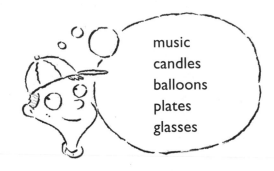

music
candles
balloons
plates
glasses

We have to have _____

➤ *Write a story about the Long's party.*

Name_____ Date _____

Faces and Places

Rewrite the caption for each U.S. president.
Use abbreviations for the names of the months.
Add the correct punctuation. Capitalize
where necessary.

1.

Born: august 10 1874

Place: west branch iowa

Born:_____

Place:_____

2.

Born: july 11 1767

Place: braintree massachusetts

Born:_____

Place:_____

3.

Born: december 5 1782

Place: kinderhook new york

Born:_____

Place:_____

4.

Born: november 23 1804

Place: hillsboro new hampshire

Born:_____

Place:_____

➤ *Record when and where you were born. Abbreviate the name of the month.*

Name_____ Date _____

What Did They Say?

Solve the picture clues for each quotation. Then rewrite the sentences using the correct punctuation and capitalization.

Example:
Sadako said, "I had a strange dream last night."
"What happened?" asked Neil.

> Use quotation marks to show the words someone says.
>
> Begin the quotation with a capital letter. Use a comma to set off a quotation from the words that tell who is speaking. If there is already a period, question mark, or exclamation point, do not add the comma.

1. jenny said 👁 8 my P's _____

_____

2. 🥫 U 🐱 ch that 🦋 🍪 asked ron _____

_____

3. bill yelled 👁 🥫 C U 🏚 _____

_____

4. Y R U in the 10 t inquired vera _____

_____

5. jasmine explained this is 4 J from K _____

_____

6. larry said 👁 🪚 2 B's _____

_____

➤ *Proofread the sentences that you wrote.*

Instant Grammar Practice Kids Will Love! Grades 4–5 Copyright © 2000, 2010 by Linda Ward Beech, Scholastic Teaching Resources

Name_____ Date _____

Talking on Paper

Fill in the empty speech balloons. On the lines below, rewrite the dialogue for both balloons using the correct punctuation and capitalization. (Dialogue follows the rules for writing quotations.) Be sure to make up a name for each character.

They're closing school for two days.

I think that's a terrible idea.

That's my chair!

_____

_____

_____

_____

_____

_____

➤ _Write more dialogue for these characters to say to each other._

Name _____ Date _____

Shortcuts

Izzy and Ozzy always repeat what each other says. Izzy, however, always uses contractions, but Ozzy never does. Fill in the speech balloons to show what Izzy and Ozzy are saying.

> Use an apostrophe to show where letters are left out in a contraction.

1. We are making soup.

2. You're going to spoil it!

3. I don't like it.

4. I will add some carrots.

5. I'm hungry.

6. That is good!

➤ *Underline the letters in Ozzy's dialogue that were left out of each contraction in Izzy's dialogue.*

Name _____ Date _____

Important Possessions

The animals are missing important parts. Complete the sentences by writing the possessive form for each animal. Use the pictures to decide if the word is singular or plural.

> To make a singular noun possessive, add an apostrophe and s ('s). To make a plural noun possessive, add an apostrophe after the s (s').

1. The _____ trunk is missing.

2. The _____ tail is gone.

3. Where are all the _____ stripes?

4. Have you seen the _____ hump?

5. The _____ spots have been misplaced.

6. The _____ antlers are not there.

7. Are the _____ manes in sight?

8. Can you find the _____ teeth?

➤ Add the missing parts to each picture.

page 6: Students' subjects, predicates, and sentences will vary.

page 7: Incomplete sentences in item 2 should be starred. Students' sentences will vary.

page 8: 1. Which star in the universe is nearest to Earth? It is the sun. 2. What is the longest bone in your body? The femur is the longest bone in your body. 3. On what continent do koalas and kangaroos live in the wild? They live in Australia.

page 9: Possible answers: 1. There's an elephant in our yard! 2. You're kidding! 3. Call the fire department! 4. Get my camera. 5. Keep the dog inside. 6. Hand me those binoculars. 7. That's quite a surprise! 8. He's sitting on my flowers.

page 10: Possible answers: 1. The harp seal pup has white fur, but adult seals have gray and brown fur. 2. Elephant seals weigh up to 8,000 pounds, and they can be as long as 23 feet. 3. Hippos are land animals, but they live in the water most of the day. 4. The killer whale may feed on smaller sea mammals, or it may eat other whales. 5. African elephants make rumbling noises to communicate, but they remain silent to warn of danger. 6. Female lions do the family hunting, and the males defend the group's territory.

page 11: 1. A statement is a sentence that tells something. It begins with a capital letter and ends with a period. 2. An exclamation is a sentence that expresses surprise or other strong emotions. It begins with a capital letter and ends with an exclamation point. 3. A compound sentence combines two or more simple sentences. Use a comma before the conjunction. 4. A command is a sentence that tells someone to do something. It begins with a capital letter and usually ends with a period. 5. A question is a sentence that asks something. It begins with a capital letter and ends with a question mark.

page 12: 1. compound sentence, statement, command, question; answer: CD or DVD 2. statement, statement, statement, question; answer: chair 3. Students' riddles and answers will vary.

page 13: 1. cowboy 2. bear 3. banana 4. computer 5. bee 6. astronaut 7.–12. Students' sentences will vary.

page 14: Students' nouns will vary but should correspond to the kinds of nouns in the key.

page 15: 1. February 2. Jerry Spinelli, Laura Ingalls Wilder, E.L. Konigsburg, Judy Blume, and Cynthia Voigt 3. Babe Ruth 4. George Washington, February 5. Valentine's Day, Sunday 6. Monday

page 16: 1. ship 2. clouds 3. Pirates 4. map 5. captain 6. rats 7. birds 8. Days 9. outlaws 10. coast 11. island 12. men 13. Treasure

page 17: sandwiches, cucumbers, radishes, cheeses, Bunches, mixes, dishes, peaches, berries, apples, cookies, candies, punches

page 18: Across—3. children 4. elves 7. halves 10. geese 11. women 13. shelves; Down—1. mice 2. knives 3. calves 5. sheep 6. oxen 8. lives 9. loaves 12. men

page 19: 1. purple things 2. things to sleep in 3. things for hair 4. beach things 5. footwear; Students' stories will vary.

page 20: Students' drawings will vary but should represent the verbs.

page 21: 1. love 2. wave 3. stare 4. smile 5. spot 6. guess; Students' sentences will vary.

page 22: Possible answers: 1. sailing 2. dance 3. walk 4. sleeps 5. shouting 6. raining

page 23: 1. Election Day comes in November. 2. Every Thanksgiving, my grandma roasts a turkey. 3. On New Year's, Nick wears a silly hat. 4. Every fall, students return to school. 5. On the Fourth of July, I march in a parade.

page 24: Possible answers: 1. Both are tools for picking up things. 2. Both are pieces of furniture to sit on. 3. Both are things to drink liquid out of. 4. Both are things worn to keep hands warm.

page 25: Across—3. found 5. became 6. won 7. cut 8. uttered 12. dug 13. dressed 14. dated; Down—1. went 2. gave 4. dotted 5. bought 7. chose 9. told 10. rode 11. drew 12. did

page 26: Change verbs to: visited, saw, called, gave, told, pushed, trampled, fell, broke, came, scared, ran, disappeared

page 27: Possible answers: will balance, will ride, will perform, will give, will sell

page 28: Possible answers: 1. This actor is talented. 2. His roles are demanding. 3. That play is a big hit. 4. Those movies are the critic's favorite. 5. Many fans are teenagers. 6. One award was really special. 7. A few fans were disappointed. 8. Acting is a real challenge.

page 29: Possible answers: 1. wiggled 2. squirmed 3. reported 4. perched 5. roared 6. fled; Students' verses will vary.

page 30: Students' answers will vary.

page 31: 1. moon 2. light 3. field 4. earth 5. earth 6. glow 7. wind 8. cornstalks 9. trees 10. silhouettes 11. sky 12. cry 13. senses 14. I 15. figures 16. call 17. enemies 18. drama 19. I 20. fire

page 32: Possible answers: 1. flowered, china mug 2. striped, silk tie 3. plaid, cotton shirt 4. old, worn-out sock 5. polka-dotted, dark sunglasses 6. square, wooden clock; Students' stories will vary.

page 33: Students' answers will vary. Make sure they use alternative adjectives.

page 34: higher, highest; more delicious, most delicious; more elaborate, most elaborate; possible answers: thick, thicker, thickest

page 35: Students' poems will vary. Make sure they use adjectives.

page 36: Possible answers: 1. eats eagerly 2. sleeps soundly 3. pours carefully 4. sits there 5. crawls around 6. barks loudly 7. will go later 8. cuts evenly

page 37: Students' sentences will vary, but should include verbs in step 2 and adverbs in step 3.

page 38: 1. They 2. he 3. her 4. me 5. She 6. him 7. I 8. us 9. It 10. them 11. us; answer: three minutes

page 39: We, It, He, we, them, She, us, He, them, him

page 40: 1. on 2. in 3. over 4. between 5. around 6. against 7. under 8. behind

page 41: Possible answers: 1. from the station before noon 2. on time in Honolulu 3. between here and there, before noon 4. by the park, on the hour

page 42: 1. I must stop at the supermarket, bakery, fruit stand, and party store. 2. I need to string the lights, buy extra ice, and set up tables. 3. I'll go to the hairdresser, shoemaker, and cleaners. 4. We have to have music, candles, balloons, plates, and glasses.

page 43: 1. Aug. 10, 1874; West Branch, Iowa 2. Jul. 11, 1767; Braintree, Massachusetts 3. Dec. 5, 1782; Kinderhook, New York 4. Nov. 23, 1804; Hillsboro, New Hampshire

page 44: 1. Jenny said, "I ate my peas." 2. "Can you catch that fly ball?" asked Ron. 3. Bill yelled, "I can see you well!" 4. "Why are you in the tent?" inquired Vera. 5. Jasmine explained, "This is for Jay from Kay." 6. Larry said, "I saw two bees."

page 45: Students' dialogue will vary.

page 46: 1. We're making soup. 2. You are going to spoil it! 3. I do not like it. 4. I'll add some carrots. 5. I am hungry. 6. That's good!

page 47: 1. elephant's 2. monkey's 3. zebra's 4. camel's 5. giraffes' 6. deer's 7. lions' 8. sharks'

48